# HIDING IN RAINFORESTS

Deborah Underwood

**www.raintreepublishers.co.uk**
Visit our website to find out more information about Raintree books.

**To order:**
☎ Phone 0845 6044371
🖷 Fax +44 (0) 1865 312263
💻 Email myorders@raintreepublishers.co.uk

Customers from outside the UK please telephone +44 1865 312262

Raintree is an imprint of Capstone Global Library Limited, a company incorporated in England and Wales having its registered office at 7 Pilgrim Street, London, EC4V 6LB – Registered company number: 6695582

Text © Capstone Global Library Limited 2011
First published in hardback in 2011
The moral rights of the proprietor have been asserted.

Edited by Rebecca Rissman and Nancy Dickmann
Designed by Joanna Hinton Malivoire
Picture research by Tracy Cummins
Originated by Capstone Global Library
Printed and bound in China by Leo Paper Products Ltd.

ISBN 978 0 431 01317 6 (hardback)
15 14 13 12 11
10 9 8 7 6 5 4 3 2 1

**British Library Cataloguing in Publication Data**
Underwood, Deborah.
  Hiding in rainforests. -- (Creature camouflage)
  1. Rain forest animals--Juvenile literature. 2. Camouflage (Biology)--Juvenile literature.
  I. Title II. Series
  591.4'72'09152-dc22

**Acknowledgements**
We would like to thank the following for permission to reproduce photographs: FLPA pp. 23, 24 (Chris Mattison); Getty Images pp. 7 (Panoramic Images) 13, 14, 29 (George Grall), 27 (Connie Coleman); Minden Pictures pp. 11, 12 (Norbert Wu); National Geographic Stock pp. 8 (Minden Pictures/Michael Patricia Fogden), 25, 26 (Minden Pictures/Mitsuhiko Imamori), 28 (Minden Pictures/Konrad Wothe); naturepl.com pp. 9, 17, 18, 19, 20 (© Pete Oxford), 15, 16 (© Nick Garbutt), 21, 22 (© Francois Savigny); Photolibrary p. 10 (John Warburton-Lee Photography); Shutterstock pp. 4 (© Map Resources), 5 (© Dr. Morley Read), 6 (© cameilia).

Cover image of a warty green burrowing frog (Scaphiophryne marmorata) camouflaged, in Madagascar, is used with permission of Naturepl.com (Edwin Giesbers).

We would like to thank Michael Bright for his invaluable help in the preparation of this book.

Every effort has been made to contact copyright holders of any material reproduced in this book. Any omissions will be rectified in subsequent printings if notice is given to the publisher.

All the Internet addresses (URLs) given in this book were valid at the time of going to press. However, due to the dynamic nature of the Internet, some addresses may have changed, or sites may have changed or ceased to exist since publication. While the author and publisher regret any inconvenience this may cause readers, no responsibility for any such changes can be accepted by either the author or the publisher.

# Contents

Some words are printed in bold, **like this**. You can find out what they mean by looking in the glossary.

# What are rainforests like?

Forests are places where trees are the main type of plant. A rainforest is a forest that gets a lot of rain. Some rainforests are warm and some are cool.

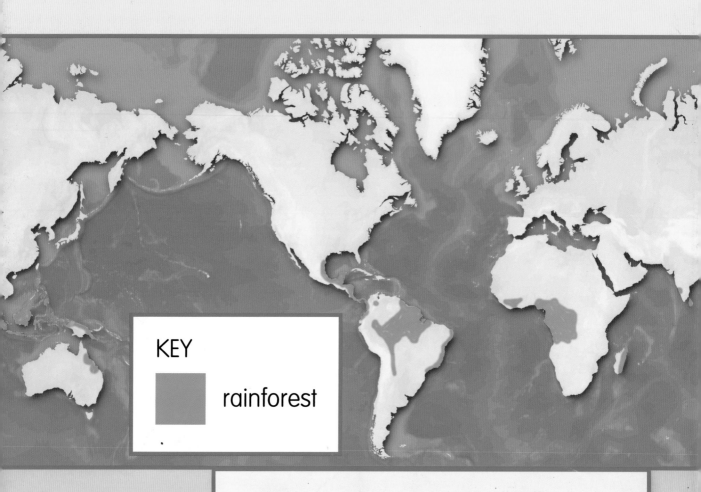

KEY

rainforest

Tropical rainforests are found in places where the weather is always warm.

Rainforests are thick forests with tall trees and many other plants.

The animals in this book live in **tropical** rainforests. Tropical rainforests are warm all the year round. Rainforests are full of food – so they are full of life!

# Living in a rainforest

Monkeys, parrots, and many other animals live in rainforests. Some live high in the trees. Others live on the ground. All rainforest animals must **survive** in a hot, wet **environment**.

Lemurs spend most of their time up in the trees.

This butterfly's wings are brown underneath. Lifting up its wings can help it hide from birds.

Rainforest animals have special **features** that help them survive in their surroundings. These features are called **adaptations**.

# What is camouflage?

**Camouflage** is an **adaptation** that helps animals to hide. The colour of an animal's skin, fur, or feathers may match the things around it.

A jaguar's spots help it to hide in the rainforest.

Caimans are related to alligators. This caiman looks like part of a log!

Animals that eat other animals are called **predators**. Camouflage makes it easier for them to hide. This helps them catch food.

Animals that **predators** eat are called **prey** animals. **Camouflage** helps them, too. A prey animal hides so it will not become a predator's meal!

What makes this chameleon blend in so well with the leaves around it?

# Find the rainforest animals

## Three-toed sloth

Some types of three-toed sloths live high in rainforest trees. Can you see how the colour of their fur helps them to **blend in**?

CAMOUFLAGED

Sloths move very slowly. They cannot run from danger. Their fur helps them to hide from **predators**, such as jaguars.

REVEALED

## Leafy katydid

When is a leaf not a leaf? When it is a leafy katydid! Animals such as bats, birds, lizards, and spiders eat katydids. A katydid's colours help it to hide from them.

CAMOUFLAGED

Some katydids are green, like leaves. Some are brown, like tree **bark**. They are active at night. During the day, katydids stay very still so they are hard to spot.

# Horned frog

Horned frogs live on the forest floor. They have two points on their heads. The frogs' colours and shape make them look like dead leaves.

CAMOUFLAGED

Horned frogs use **camouflage** when they catch food. A frog stays very still until **prey** passes by. Then the frog shoots out its sticky tongue and gobbles up the prey!

REVEALED

## Leaf-tailed gecko

A leaf-tailed gecko can flatten its body against a tree. Its tail is shaped like a leaf. This lets the gecko hide while it sleeps.

The tail helps the gecko in another way, too. If a **predator** grabs a gecko's tail, the tail drops off. This lets the gecko escape! Then the gecko grows a new tail.

REVEALED

# Imperial moth

The imperial moth has a clever way of hiding in a rainforest. It looks just like a leaf! When it stays still, it disappears amongst the leaves on the forest floor.

An imperial moth does not eat when it is an adult. Other animals might try to eat it, though! The moth's shape and colour help it to hide from hungry animals.

REVEALED

## Great potoo

Potoo birds hunt at night and sleep during the day. Potoos have feathers that look like tree **bark**. This helps the sleeping birds stay safe.

If danger comes near, potoos close their eyes. They point their beaks up to the sky. This makes the potoos look even more like pieces of a tree!

eats other insects. It sits _ to pass by. Then the _ _rev_ with its front legs.

## Reticulated python

Reticulated pythons are the world's longest snakes. They can be over 9 metres long! Can you see how the python's skin **pattern** helps it **blend in**?

CAMOUFLAGED

REVEALED

Sometimes a python hunts by hiding in a tree. Its **camouflage** helps it hide. When **prey** passes below, the python catches it. Then it swallows the prey whole.

## Orchid mantis

The orchid mantis looks l
legs are shaped like peto
to spot a mantis on a pla

ard

Th

CAMOUFLAGED

and we...
mantis grabs the pre...

REVEALED

This owl monkey's fur helps it hide in rainforest trees.

The rainforest is full of **camouflaged** animals. If you are ever lucky enough to visit a rainforest, look closely. You never know what you might see!

# Animals that stand out

Some types of birds of paradise live on the island of New Guinea. There are few large **predators** on the island. So the birds do not need to hide.

Male birds of paradise have bright colours that help them attract mates.

The blue poison arrow frog stands out in the rainforest.

Poison arrow frogs have **poisons** in their skin. Their bright colours warn animals not to eat them. The frogs come in many colours. Some are red with blue legs. They are called blue jeans frogs!

# Glossary

**adaptation** special feature that helps an animal survive in its surroundings

**bark** tough, outer part of a tree trunk

**blend in** matches well with the things around it

**camouflage** adaptation that helps an animal blend in with its surroundings

**environment** place where an animal lives

**feature** special part of an animal

**pattern** shapes and marks on an animals skin, fur, or feathers

**poison** something dangerous that can make you very ill, or even kill you

**predator** animal that eats other animals

**prey** animal that other animals eat

**survive** stay alive

**tropical** place that is very warm all the year round

# Find out more

## Books to read

*Animals: A Children's Encyclopedia*
  (Dorling Kindersley, 2008)

*Essential Habitats: Tropical Rainforest Habitats*,
  Barbara Taylor (TickTock Media Ltd., 2009)

*Focus on Habitats: Rainforest Animals*,
  Stephen Savage (Wayland, 2006)

## Websites

**www.bbc.co.uk/nature/habitats/Tropical_and_
subtropical_moist_broadleaf_forests**
A BBC website where you can watch films and find
out more about your favourite rainforest animals.

**www.nhm.ac.uk/kids-only/life/life-jungle**
Discover more fascinating facts about rainforests on
the Natural History Museum's Kids Only website.

# Index